Graveyards On Other Planets

Roberto Pastore

Parthian, Cardigan SA43 1ED
www.parthianbooks.com
First published in 2025
© Roberto Pastore 2025
ISBN 978-1-917140-58-4
Editor: Susie Wildsmith
Cover design by Lyn Davies Design
Cover image: 'Tela Habitada [Inhabited Canvas]' by Helena Almeida (1976).
Photographer: Mário de Oliveira, CAM-Centro de Arte Moderna Gulbenkian, Lisboa.
Typeset by Elaine Sharples
Proofread by Harper Dafforn
Printed and bound by 4edge Limited, UK
Published with the financial support of the Books Council of Wales
British Library Cataloguing in Publication Data
A cataloguing record for this book is available from the British Library
Printed on FSC accredited paper

How beautiful they are, the trains you miss!

– Jules Laforgue

CONTENTS

Prologue

vultures circle

blood scents the air

regardless I walk my beating heart to the arena

The Great Flood

This was January 2005 in Carlisle. I was
living with Louise at the time, above some
shops. I'd look out the window
at night & see people urinating
in the shop fronts.
It turned me on, honestly.
5am we'd be woken by
the loading vans & the pigeons.
Brutish grey mornings, each one
the same as the last, until
this one morning when
I looked out the window & watched
a man in a canoe row down Scotch St.
The rain had been heavy the night before &
had flooded all the way to the horizon. I was
elated. No work. A few hours later
the power went out all over
the city; no water, no gas. It was
January and dark by
early afternoon, 4pm there was
nothing to do but go to sleep.
The next day was the same, we
fucked on the sofa while families were
evacuated from their homes
not far from us. It was glorious.

The day before the flood, on some inspired whim
I'd bought a six-pack of
San Pellegrino. This was a huge extravagance
& something I'd never done before

or since, but there it was,
call it a premonition or just dumb luck,
but we had water. Bert, you were
born blessed, I told myself.
The only thing was no coffee or tea
because we couldn't heat the water. By this
time the flood itself had receded a bit,
so I walked to the centre opposite
the tourist office where they'd set up
vans & tents. I spoke to a woman in
a cagoule who said I could get water & shelter
in the church if I needed it. I didn't.
By day three the toilet was pretty rank
as it wouldn't flush. There was something so
tender about our combined shit & piss though, the way
they were so different even though we'd eaten
the same food. Until then I'd
never met any of my neighbours
from down the corridor but
by day three we were all on a first
name basis, all of us concerned that this
might end soon & we'd have to
go back to work. The guy in the flat
next door died soon after this
from an electrical fire, but
on this day we were two floors up & alive.
More alive than
we'd been for some time.
I had some tea lights.
It took over an hour, but I boiled
that pan of sparkling Italian mineral water
by holding it over as many candles as I had
& we had coffee that day.
It felt like magic, that. Please understand,

3

we had no way of knowing
the extent of the disaster. No news,
no phone signal, nothing. No one had any clue.
Some of my friends lost everything.

Something else happened.
That afternoon I decided
to go for a walk to see how far back
the water had receded, so I opened
the door of the flat
& as I took a step into
the corridor a light came on
just above my head. Took
another step, another light came on.
Each new light lit my passage along that corridor
& by the time I reached the door to
the stairwell, all the lights were on.
I opened the front door & walked out
into the arcade, it was dark & there
was no one else around. I watched
the streetlights ping on
one by one. Light!
Light everywhere!
As though I'd been the one
to bring it. As though I alone had been
witness to the miracle.
I felt the power surge through me
as the whole city lit up.

The Scarecrow Observes A Nubbin In The Field

That time in the Serpent Café
she put her hands palm down on the table
palms down like that
as the sterile light
seeped in
lit her jaw and
throat, where she had a rash
looked like razor burn.

She laid her hands
on the varnished surface,
among the cups and serviettes, the debris of
a long cold afternoon turning over
the same old ground

and, counting her fingers,
she found only nine.

The Cloak

When the imprint of the unnamed hand
fades on the yellow sheet, I go out,
frail as an old wing, to get closer.
In my rucksack a loaf of bread,
prayer book, painkillers, and the woolly hat
I bought at Green Man years ago.
Around my shoulders the cloak of leaving
with the mucus still on its hem.

I make a path between hoofprints and demon root,
the purple eyeballs of the cabbage. To the city
where I first cut my tongue on the superhighway.
Where I first saw the hand
that stitched the cloak, and wrote about it
with my bubblegum-pink nib.

It's nice here
beneath the oak tree, listening to
the cars go by. May they make it home safely, and may
you also be safe,
as eyes under coins, or American flags. May you
bask in Summer's beehiving belly
while I put on the cloak,
whose weight is the measure of days.

Here I am vomit off
the rollercoaster. Here I do poke myself in the eye.
Here I wore my hairshirt to the nightclub,
but I don the cloak of horsehair tonight.
Here I worshipped the blotchy skin of a school crush.

Here, the wild onions of her dreams.
Here I did put on boxing gloves and punch the sun
to get her attention. Here I was pus on your
mirror, lord. Here I jack-knifed the seed.
Here I will lay down the cloak, to sleep
beneath your twinkling spores.

When the imprint of the unnamed hand
fades on the yellow sheet, I go out,
frail as an old wing, to get closer.

A Worm On The Horizon

Across the fields
the distance awakens from its
                    dream of him.
The way his thighs looked against white sheets,
the moth-eyed fear in the night.
His bed was the outside world
climbing into you.

He proposed out of guilt.
On your honeymoon you stood in the sea
                    for the first time.
Beneath the blue sky
the loss took root.

And now, as one visiting a grave
more from habit than grief,
                    you gaze
at the ground, at your feet,
and see the new bruise of the earth
begin to rise.

The Years In White

Continually in these poems
I find my hand reaching out
    to the cold room
    where we burned.

The years
in white
begin to speck.

Years
    of walking along corridors
    trying each door
    climbing stairs & taking elevators

knowing only longing & september
    calling out all the wrong names

seeing only what stays behind.

It has always been this way for me,
even as the half-remembered houses stretch
    & bend
    it is my own room I am locked out of

my own name
that privately I reach for.

On The Windowsill Facing East
She Left A Cigarette Burning

and as the sun rose from behind the mountain
I watched the smoke pirouette into the clean winter light
and saw
Yvonne Rainer's hands
          disembodied
     indestructible
sculpting the newborn air.

Speaking Of Failure...

Michelangelo abandoned his first Risen Christ
in a rage when the marble revealed
a black vein across Christ's left cheek,
like Lance Henriksen.

My grandfather, who
only ever wore a white vest and was, I think,
a Fascista and a poacher, also had a scar just like that.

Not much heals, or even gets punished.
Time keeps retreating from
the scene of its crimes. Some call that Mercy.
I don't.

As key takes
the form of hole, so
the hare's heart is unlocked
by my grandfather's shotgun.

Hole which light burnt through, as life
festers the centre of all things,
so the savage yolk emulsifies.
Night remains day,
as I remain
   apprentice to myself.

An eye at the base of the horizon
where pours in the box of colours, everything
   begins to scramble, the secret that kept you hidden.
A donut the shape of Christ's hand, a cup of steaming coffee,

and it's April again.
(from *aperire*, meaning *to open*).
The last party I went to was a downer; it had
    neither a beginning or an end.
The last time I saw death I asked for forgiveness,
    held the fading heart in my hand
    and listened
to a world inchoate as words written down in a hurry,
never arriving at their purpose,
    the part where the wound rushes
    towards the bullet.

Old-Fashioned Prayer To Her Seventh House

In the church of the Sacro Cuore di Gesù
I spilt blood into the holy water
a rabbit's heart in my hand.
The groundskeeper's daughter
was a year ahead of me in school.
I was 16; had been living my life wholly as confessor
and priest as though it were
a conversation with myself.
Her name was Gloria
whenever she walked in the room it was like
the air around me grew gelatinous
like slippery elm.
Her father tended to the graves
tumorous flowers of his cheeks damp with sweat
dirty stains on his red shirt
where he'd wipe his hands.
I broke down
I remembered a woman rocking me on her knee.
Through the stained glass it looked as though he'd
sliced off his nipples with those long shears
and was bleeding out.
I'll wear them as cufflinks, I thought
I'll take out his daughter and bury dust in the earth
I'll take her in the fields
I'll stalk the outer darkness of this longing.

Everything Is Named, Everything Is Counted

Through old windows I still see
    your long red hair
it covers the stones & the rain & the grey towers
    even now
    I see in your hand
mint & rosemary you have picked
    & all the shame of my life
    like a bell
    ringing itself at your feet
I should have
    raised you as my child
    though you were older than me
    & the years had no human voice
I would shoot myself
    in the space above my temple
    where I rise into you
    where the winds rise
& car alarms sound & dogs vomit red hair
    sprays of unreachable red hair
    into the night
    into the memory of night
where the shepherd looks out
    & sees you
    through the long resonance of old windows.

Red Telescope

Remember the red telescope
and how you used to kneel
on top of the sofa and point it
at the night sky,
so disappointing, wasn't it –
how distant the moon still seemed
and how, through the eye piece
it felt almost further away,
somehow less convincing.
Silently, you felt the distance expand
inside you
then you'd feel yourself discorporate,
implicated by the watchful blackness
until, out of dread, you'd tilt it down
into the neighbour's windows
where the urgency of their human bodies
moving about, cooking, undressing,
doing human things under yellow light
felt rapturous,
so intimate you could almost convince yourself
they were consenting, that this was
a performance
just for you, a secret they were
letting you in on –
little one,
what is shown is not seen,
what is seen is not shown.

I See Her Now In A Blue Dwarf Star

The first sighting
was outside the newsagents where she used to smoke
   so she began as smoke rising.
It was a Monday night   the dogs of Leighton Buzzard
sensing danger from her, began barking.
The dogs barked & the sirens blared at the days of her,
long gone. Chemtrails of her
above the house where she used to live
   now a relic to her ascendency.

Am I mythologising her, is this not
how it all went down?
Was I not
also disappearing?

The chronology is a sequence of events each rejecting
the precursor.
Reject metaphor; metaphor is a cheap trick.
Her flesh awakened to earth, then remembered it was smoke
   the continuous beat of her
   a pollution
   a pulse that could be heard
emanating
from the allotment at night
faint   but regular.
Uterine contractions, blood
lifting into trees, coating Linslade tunnel with blood.

To be so full of something and not
   be able to speak it.

The death of her came first,
precursor to public outcry.
Blocked were   the bronchial alleyways
clairvoyant drone circling
   a violet sky
transmitting relentless bombardment of children.
The satellite images show only heaving confectionery,
mouth holding only phantoms of Dresden.

I wanted to ask her friends about her   to hold a
séance or construct a shrine but
it's no good, half of them are alcoholics & I want them to
have a good time – we all lost some form of her
when she became rubble.
After the schools & hospitals were bombed
we looked into our own hearts & minds & knew
we were
irretrievable.

But you can't just pack up & leave, you need
to keep those feet on this earth somehow.

Don't ask me what metaphors I'd use; I only know
that language is telepathic & can be made to stretch
but I believe the omens of the half-moon
the hierophant
   twelve slashes on the trunk of the cherry tree
   her heart tuned to a diatonic scale
& outside Asda, Vivian wound down
her car window to warn me of
   'a coming storm'
which I alone would witness, & I thought it might
be you.

Croker's Mountains

It's a strange kind of dissonance, being told
that the thing you're seeing isn't there.
We go about our days
with the dull guilt of the firing squad.

The desert
once fell in love with a lion.

Meanwhile the gentle are forced to lie facedown
in their own blood. Trees are hung with genitals
that the sun dries and beautifies.

The throats of swans are wrung while engines
catch & wheeze. The sun rises. We pass it on like
a gift
regifted.

Nash Point

if you were to let out a halloo here at night
it would give the illusion of finitude; of having edges

your voice would come back
as though returned from some errand

and were you to stand close enough to the centre, you might also stand
within yourself, sturdy as a horse, or

like a porpoise, you might pick up the distant echo of
something startling; the point at which your voice rebounded off

the sky – but we know the sky doesn't end – it only retreats
from whatever feels furthest from itself

The Last Day

On the First Day, even the stone house
   in its frost
   seemed new
abandoned loves crackled
   beneath feathery rime
   where leaf & grass & time held still
you were young & predestined
black tea & hot porridge
   a view of the mountain
   a view of the white earth.

On the Second Day, a knock at the door
   awoke you
   with its metallic rap
worms nudged blackberries
   prolapsed & sunburnt
   from last summer
you lay in bed & prayed for night
but there was no night, only
   the call of the magpie
   the call of its sharp need.

On the Third Day, your father
   appeared in his chair
   his black fingers pointing
at the window, out the window
   from the bottom of the well
   a voice was forming, birdlike
wrought from grime & rainwater
his silence had filled your life & now, oh listen
   as the gaping hole breathes
   so the gaping hole stinks.

On the Fourth Day, a friendly young man
    appeared in the garden
    smelling of hawthorn
carrying a suitcase full of old knives
    mud on his boots
    hard eyes smiling
a new light inside the mountain
even the unseen & the unwelcome began to stir
    the fly on the urinal
    altar of moth larvae.

On the Fifth Day, a tower of discharge
    rose up from
    the mountain's heaving core
your father & the over-friendly young man
    led you blindfolded
    to the dining table
golden roast potatoes boiled sprouts stuffing & peas
soft breezes on lace curtains, oh sharpening knives!
    Some days you are the main course
    some days soup.

On the Last Day, impossible to see the house now
    beyond the diamond light
    shining mould of blown seed & flesh
each bird had overfed, grown so heavy they
    could not fly –
    they are at the bottom of the well
you rose from the green earth inside a jelly
on hands & knees you crawled
    in love with the burning shore
    in love with shit & stars.

Out Of Your Life

you fall out of your life, then

you catch
   yourself

inside your life again

one moment removed,
                 the next
immersed

     among life
        excluded from it

and so it goes, without
   cause or seemingly

explanation

as if the interior were
   translation

of some exterior reality

some say fear
some say ecstasy

you fall out of your life

then you
   catch yourself

Missing

Another cat gone missing, this one not mine.
It's November,
    a goodbye train

moves through us. We make
the mewing sounds, check the bins, the
back alleys.

It's a nerve-wracking business.
We end up
stalking our own absences, trailing
our own
    missing cat

through the softening shelters of our own bodies.

Seven Disappearances

I.
I think about Steven Carrington
and his tragically mishandled character arc
and how, after nearly dying
in that explosion in Season Two,
after all that reconstructive surgery,
he was surprised that his eyes
were the same colour.

II.
In the doctor's waiting room
I overhear a little girl talking with her nan:

they cut me open
and what did they find inside?
there was blood.
blood everywhere?
no, blood just somewhere.

III.
More than 10,000 human bodies   what is being called
a 'shadow death toll'   thought missing in Gaza.
Buried beneath buildings   detained
while fleeing   no way for the hospitals to keep
a record of them all.

I google 10.000 people statistics   find an article
called 'Visualizing Crowd Sizes' it says: we need a stadium
to hold an audience this big   and I try to
picture a stadium   in which no one
has shown up for the game.

IV.

It is permissible, as an alternative to destruction by fire, for documents to be packed in weighted crates and dumped in very deep and current-free water at maximum practicable distance from the coast*

And somewhere 2000 fathoms deep
a placenta undreams itself   in a lightless flowering
a new god   sways in wreaths of algae   gills strut
breath of water   seabones hum in fishfat flapdoodle   teeth
hard in their jewels gnash mulish   for a taste of this world.

V.

I am nine years old and I've been constipated for days.
Mum & Dad drive me to the hospital and
as we pull into the car park
'(Something Inside) So Strong' plays on the car radio.

VI.

Upon seating herself in the chair, I informed her that I had the power to cause her to disappear.**

The Vanishing Lady trick is
an illusion of transportation, not disappearance.
She always comes back,
either in the same chair or somewhere in the gallery.
Sometimes she appears as a skeleton, before
coming back a woman.

V.

I think about Granger Taylor
who built a spacecraft and claimed
to be in communication with aliens through his CB radio
and who, in November 1980
disappeared

after leaving a note for his parents which said
I have gone away to walk aboard an alien spaceship.

03/24

---

* Instruction to dispose of thousands of documents archiving British colonial brutality in at least 23 countries and territories; a programme known as Operation Legacy.
** From magician Charles Bertram's autobiography *Isn't It Wonderful?*

Venus Infers

I'm getting used to the night again
and the feeling of falling behind. Co-op's shut, but
the stockroom lights make the street feel homely,
as the rain taps away on the old sins and the peeling phone box.
Years ago, when the styles were different,
we walked differently in the rain,
it was something you could count on
to upholster the boredom and dust. These days
I'm just dusty and bored. Waiting
for a salvation history to make sense
of it all. I attend the reunion of myself.
Swapping out lime water for chamomile tea.
Comb-over days in which we refuse to accept what is lost.

If the dogs need my blessing, if the unseen voice
needs my blessing, if the wild sea needs my blessing, well, alright.
Mercury elucidates what Venus only infers –
that the soil must inevitably become a bed
though only in the sense that it will be a place where
we grow stuff,
not necessarily a place where we sleep.
Those in the know say we are at the beginning of an era
which has not yet been defined
and, according to the old mythological and cosmological project,
those who are alive at a given time are invited to be
agents of transformation
in the ongoing invention of the future.
I turn on the record player, watch it spin.

Speaking of clichés – earlier today, in the record store, I overheard
someone say that time is a construct.
Well, yes,
but it's a convincing one.
Reality may be only a prosthetic, but
all is spiral to longing.
The moon was always fattest
over the Piazza San Ferdinando di Puglia, where my dad first
met my mum, when she was 16.
My mother tells me how she laughed on the night of their wedding,
at the sight of the white sheet laid out
to soak up her first blood (that old Italian patriarchal cliché).
She was on her period anyway so they soaked
that sheet bloody and found it funny and I try to
imagine that; the two of them laughing, and young.

Youth was no great shakes anyway. Now look at me;
I am no one
watching you wanting more. All the resonances of
life still arouse me, the fear
of death dances in my scrotal memory, saying *Kiss me with
an accent! Do it again for the first time!* One thing I know;
we must devote ourselves, with some conviction, to
the construct. Because, and I can vouch for this,
when you start to perceive
the rules by which you've chosen to govern your own life
as unreal, you become a monster. I'm getting used
to the night, it's alright really.
Stay still, I tell it. *Become light.* I sleep
with one earbud in,
the sound of voices comforts me.

I Am Speaking To You Now

I opened my eyes and saw the arbour outside
and you kneeling above me

kiss of life you gave with thick salty lips crucifix
       dangling against
    tanned skin
coarse beard the colour of dead grass

      with your hand
    upon hand
you brought the breath of air

my first immortelle
first gravestone.

That Place On Oswald Street

I remember
    walking in on you;
you were sat on the white chair.

    It seemed to me
    that you

were falling
      forward, or out, or
         apart.

Along your vein where the
    lamplight
    faintly glowed

I watched the dandelion bloom.

The Cat Unscratch

It comes back to you. The old fire, the fever for it,
the self-eclipsing delight. Out of
the blue, it reappears.
Or it doesn't. For many, it doesn't.
Some people barely had it to begin with. Traded it
in without even knowing they had it, and what for?
Acceptance, or ambition, or because they didn't
know what else to do, the years
piled up over them like thick blankets
made them tired
forgetful
dysmorphic
and, caught unawares, their barriers
down, they gave in to the security of the
old narratives, lost what
made them feel alive to begin with, again I'm asking
what for?
The usual things,
sometimes it's the smallest things.
You start dividing your life into pieces, you start talking
like they do:
company talk, small talk, broscience, gb news; fascism.
Be vigilant. If you don't succumb to it, you can reclaim what is yours.
Stay true to the source & it will never truly abandon you.
It will come to you again
that good ache
sad heartsong.
It belongs to you.
Don't trade it in for the hand on your shoulder, a promotion at the job
that's killing you, the accolades of peers

you've no respect for,
the loneliness of the staff party.
It returns. Like a cat or an erection, the gut-churning
bad dream, the old agonies & joys. Hold on
to it. If you lose everything else, hold onto this.
It will keep you
sane
while death dances its
slow dance
backstage.

Supplication On Behalf Of Lucio

Maybe we only wanted to see the ocean
surrounded by the hard black night
as, along the autostrada, the drone of hot traffic
steadily loosened the shale, the jutting outcrops
that glowed above the beating waves seemed
lit from within.

The same light meets us now
in separate cities in separate lives, so distant that
when I speak to the local men here their eyes
remind me of that same sea rendered ulterior.

Your palm cradled the flame as you
brought it to the tip of your cigarette, it was so tender
you'd never know that earlier that day
those same hands slit bellies open in the markets
as the sun baked down on your bloodstained vest.

It was holy, where what is holy remains
in the imprint of the unaccountable.
In the cut of, or swift release of, your pocketknife
with which you cleaved the stone in half
and with your half, as we listened
to the turning ocean, you partial eclipsed the moon.

I re-enact the doglike way you scratched your wrist
against the coarse stubble of your jaw; I do it now as I sit watching
the sun climb the Irish Sea.
As the dog walkers and joggers fall endlessly from
the white cliff into the night of those nine days

when we lay down in darkness, the holy darkness of the Adriatic
and pooled our cash and talked of our fathers.

Lucio, where are you if not beside me now?
Your books gathering dust in the corner,
your teeth in the handkerchief,
your old man still running from the lit fuse,
your mouth hesitating on the exhale.

Morning Thought

the bleat in the still meadow

language hexes
even that which cannot be touched.

words
become object, have
physicality,

drive their nails into the unseen.

Freedom To Stay

I don't like to think about it much anymore
but before I invented a prototype for love &
constructed a persona around it, I was a
good boy, devoted to fog & bad advice & friendship.
I was taught to split myself in two, & I gave
all of what was deemed good to you, & all
of what I knew to be my true self
to Kirsten. I would catch the train to Leighton Buzzard
and look out the train window
at the fields & flatlands thinking
about her neck, the way her hair
curled inwards against it & seemed to lap against it
like the sea.
Meanwhile you took me to the coast
and I got sunburnt & spent the night in the bathtub
and you were upset because (& I had no clue about this) you'd
planned the whole thing so we'd finally fuck.
But Kirsten had the softest, just the
softest chestnut brown hair I'd ever seen. I remember her in
a black polo neck in The Bedford Arms, drinking vodka & coke,
that neck
of hers hidden but
the knowledge of it, the lean milkwhite knowledge of it drove me
wild. This was the era of alt-country, the notion of
authenticity was big,
which I suppose, looking back, was a last stand for that kind of thing.
I was invested in the moment & would watch
a lot of westerns unironically, listened
to George Jones, listened to 'Freedom To Stay' by Waylon Jennings
a lot. Went to see Lambchop live where they played 'Caterpillar'

& listened to 'Blue' by Lucinda Williams & felt it.
You could still smoke indoors & the pub would
have this beautiful blue cloud hovering over everyone and
music blaring & the loud chatter of people crammed in
& sweating & pushing past each other. Beautiful odour of
sweat & nicotine. You took me round the back
of the beer garden
to explain something to me, something which I already
knew. I hated him & the fact that you could
somehow simultaneously like us both & that I had to
share that hallowed space in your
heart, or head, or body, with him – I didn't want us both to be there.
So I didn't say a word, just turned tail
back inside & grabbed Kirsten's hand & we walked all
night together around those muggy September streets
& alleys & back gardens, & all night we held hands
& kissed & talked about whatever was going on with
us at that time & I never wanted it to end, just like
this poem, I wanted to trap it in amber, like that,
because I knew tomorrow this would all hurt & I'd be full
of regret & oh god save us from the mornings & how
daylight hardens the edges of things which appear
soft at night, how daylight makes us
aware of the stains & dust & bad pores of life & how time
does that too,
so I'm just going to leave us there in the dark,
leaning in to smell the night smells, the Impulse
in her armpits, walking under
streetlights our young bodies pumping blood
as if nothing else mattered,
as if only the heart ruled.

Born To This

The red-lipped batfish yawns,
flowers spit bleach
as the still-burning sun drifts off to sleep.

What if we were are all virgins again,
suddenly
all that hell to parry.
The awful potential of us all.

I get up from the bed, pull the shade.

Born to this,
a wild terrifying maggot
reduced to flab & horn & you & I &
the rubix of love & angel-snot & the fallowing heart
the whiplash memory the unstoppable train of thought
the slackening grip the ingrowing hair the recurring dream
the things that shine the things that pirouette the things that
contract the measuring of time the floodtide
the chariot the punctured tire the blood on the toilet paper
the not-quite-near-enough the not-quite-removed-enough the revival of
youthful spirit the canon recoils the goddamn boredom
of it all the not ever knowing why it all was.

Mania

As if I needed to be reminded the night can't see me
I go out to look at it.

Once I was
flat on my back
   with my brother   patch of grass
alongside
Mentmore Rd.

When we were teenagers   and drunk   and when
   each new thing
    was an awakening.

Interminable then   the waiting years
holding us
back.

I knew the mania of the fly
violently throwing itself at the world

only to be
defeated

by something
inconceivable as glass.

Passing Through These Scenes With You

I approach you in the conventional way
   my hand outstretched
as though I were handing you a ticket
   usher of my blood!
   May you forever look back
at this moment to trace an absence.

All that you have been working on
all this tireless pursuit of pleasure
   is already lost.
Lead me into the darkened theatre.

This is how the world turns
only halfway – lassoed by gravity, seduced
   by the touch of stars.

Rats go scurrying into the night and I
   write my sad poems
   to your engagement finger. You sing so beautifully
as all around
the cone of your spotlight
   my heart performs
   the wall of death perpendicular.

Passing through these scenes with you
death seems only
a thing on the horizon, or is it just
   grit in my eye?

The dead are always only missing
and so
    remain glamorous
      remain vital
as ceaselessly they mock our
lack of style
our faith in the three acts:

anticipation
apprehension
slime.

No One Wants To Hear It

I've heard it said – or was it sung?
– that you're twice as shy after you've
been bitten & that the devil you know
is better than the devil you don't know.

I won't tell you about the dream I had –

it was all satellite dishes & shell suits.
The weekend was never far away.

I don't know the devil.

Never been bit.

Don't Be A Stranger

I pass you in the act of natural early evening light,
when the branch-like urges reach up & reach
out. I pass you
in the practice of my own lonely migrations. You are
your own only obstacle.
I pass you waiting for someone's love, stake in hand,
the sun sets & I pass, the abandoned playground with one
red shoe, & I go by
singing 'Who Am I' by Country Joe & The Fish.
Think of me, when your thoughts turn to regret.
Think of me, please, with grace, anytime.
Think of me, when you're spinning on the dancefloor.
Think of me, without end.
I pass fountains of clear cool water on my way, I pass
the bluefly & the buzzard, soggy newspaper & electronic dials,
the snoops, snipers, skinnydippers, I pass
the halfdream of youth, & I pass us as teenagers too trippy &
unwieldy for this world.
& I pass the relics of whiteness, everywhere, & the
fallen leaves;
leapfrogging the overly fond of themselves, I wave them
goodbye & sing the old
Christmas songs, I sing them smiling because they are beautiful,
I am always waving goodbye.
I pass seedlings & pollen & mossy graves. I step over birches
& facemasks & faultlines. I speak to rising waters
& loneliness &
cancer. I am all ears to all flesh & unflesh, all loves & unloves
& I grow taller with
each step, my feet swollen & gross in my dank espadrilles.

I keep walking, think of me doing my walkies, think of
me magnanimously,
neither dark nor light academia. Think of me drowning, or
walking on water,
think of me no longer among you. Then I will be nothing &
still be something without end, when that
last day of me comes, oh & the
whole air just did a sigh thinking of it.

I Read Your Poems

I'm sorry, I couldn't help myself.
I found them when you went out for something
in an old box stuffed with schoolwork
and certificates, under your stairs.
I did like them, mostly
but was a bit put out to find
no mention of me at all.
Funny, all these years
I thought I'd been the boy
who broke your heart the first time.

Mountain Song

The climb is further
than these four walls,
to arrive at the idea of the mountain.

You send down spit, from the precipice
of the afternoon, as your socks dry
on the idea of the radiator.

Thataway

Tonight I believe it's goodbye.
The rain slicks the black courtyard & I feel it,
a muted minor chord – not unlike the
heart's own coda – falling like a long blue dress
over the cul-de-sac &, why not, the whole entire world.

I ran away from this town
or, okay – if you want to get into it
– I chased your everextinguishingflame out of here.
But this is the room I grew up in, alone
& watched you pass from this vantage point;
my narrow tush on the sill, yours out there on Mentmore Rd.
The glass fogged up. Impossibly hopefilled candles were lit.

It's a concern, this habit of mine.
It's like trying to follow the path of
      a
             single
          drop
   of
      rain
    in
           a
             rainstorm
impossible to get a fix on it.
The serpentine maze of our...
                well, us.

& tonight I'm starting to believe this goodbye.
Can we discount the utter thoughtlessness of

our twenties, skip those
barren years between?
Tend this dusty earthsagging corona
that has a certain
rugged beauty now.

Was there ever that much to it?
You took my hand, I took yours,
down Aglionby Street & Warwick Road we marched like
cartoon mice into whatever fateless night,
under that wretched fucking moon. Can we at least
keep in touch, I said,
like pathetic ex-lovers sometimes do?

We didn't, but anyway.
I have come full-circle, my forehead against glass,
these fingerprint smudges you eventually knew.

It is raining still, listen,
would you sometimes think of me
in your weaker moments, y'know,
in this unexpected middle-age that's the most we get to ask for.

It's long past goodbye, I suppose – it's just that I'm always, even now, still,
going nowhere, looking over my shoulder
at you & everything else
going thataway.

In A Wetherspoons In The Early Oughts I Make A Confession To Myself Only

I'm trying to convince you of something.

I'll admit I used to enjoy the student gossip
& I still miss your mohawk, the felt-tip red of it.

Oh! Wetherspoons in the early oughts!

Teething century of dread.
You had a stud in your nose & the boy
came up to your chin.

The rain & wonder of it all. The old
cinema on Botchergate, men in hoodies selling us baggies
& back down along the road for a vision of the eclipse.
It was varnished tables & loose change & indie landfill & your fingernails
peeling the labels as the machines lit up. I wanted
to touch your mouth with my sad young mouth.

If I was lonely there was no one to blame
but GOD.

I needed a friend, it's true
& you
were so pale.
I'd sit & listen to your punky Irish beef, wishing
I was your type. I would've taken you to the wall.

The pigeons were in bad shape on that street in that moment in
history. Possibly the bus stop was a toxic environment.

The noise
distracting to them
& in the afternoons as the lights came on, before the offices closed & the
schools let out, that lull
held me in a place I have never fully left.

There were these two crafty little speedfreaks, adorable
skilled raconteurs to which I succumbed. Told myself the good things,
like yourself, belonged to
other people. Told myself you had better options
than this jittery Catholic boy of some notoriety.

Your fingers were long & thin. Tried to picture
them just now.

Gently asked GOD for them.
GOD who had abandoned me sometime around 2001.

I wanted you. I made that clear in that moment
but silently & to myself, I watched the sun set a beautiful pink mauve on
the dirty mirror
as yet another day climbed out of reach.

Pure Bunting

Let me be forgotten
like the weather, or a song
on the radio.
A barely remembered sunset
in some foreign
country, one summer
...long ago.

I was the dregs of your life,
pure bunting.
The lightest of breezes brushing your
cheek, one afternoon
while you were
half asleep.

No Other

After all of this is done,
    & I stand
    on the summit, overlooking
the silver city,

I'll take my walk among the dead.

As the earthworm & snail alight from
the stone, the soil in reverence winks back.
It was unlike anything else.

    It was a house.

I'll tell them
as I pass by

I loved everything in that house.

I changed the tire, made a note
to try Henderson's Relish. The Post Office was bleak.
It felt real enough, although
life often
had the background quality of a laugh-track.

I will remember how evening fell, alongside you.

A light so clean, it burns
all the details away.

I won't miss me,
only my other self –

    the one
    who kept me company.

The Snake Waves Its Hands

On a day the same as any other
you perform the new act,
        astonished
         at its effortlessness
the way it was just
there
      something in the periphery

waiting to be had.

The light catches your life,
you turn.

Notes

'Oh! qu'ils sont pittoresques les trains manqués!': Jules Laforgue was a Franco-Uruguayan symbolist poet, an early exponent of free verse (*vers libre*). There are several existing translations and variations of this line from *Derniers Vers* (1965), but my favourite, the one I've used, is from a song from 1971 called 'The Magic Wasn't There' by Julie Covington, written by Pete Atkin and Clive James.

The Great Flood: On January 8th, 2005, nine inches of rain fell in 24 hours across Carlisle and North Cumbria. It was the worst flood that region has seen for 200 years. Three people were killed: Margaret Threlkeld, Margaret Porter and Michael Scott.

On The Windowsill Facing East She Left A Cigarette Burning: Yvonne Rainer choreographed 'Trio A' in 1966 and performed it for camera in 1978. In her poem also titled 'Trio A' she writes 'the forward momentum/of practice/of object/no ritual here/the weight of the body/is material proof/that air is matter/and mind's married to muscle'. (Rainer, Yvonne. 2011. *Poems*. Brooklyn, NY. 9: Badlands Unlimited).

Croker's Mountains: In 1818 an ill-fated Arctic expedition to discover the Northwest Passage, led by Commander John Ross, was cut short when Ross insisted a non-existent range of mountains blocked their way. He named the range, which no one could see, Croker's Mountains. It's unclear if this was an hallucination, a mirage caused by weather conditions, or if he just made them up because he wanted to go home.

Seven Disappearances:

I: Steven Carrington was a character in the television series *Dynasty*. One of the first gay characters on American TV, he would eventually become bisexual and marry two women. He was originally played by Al Corley, who was replaced by Jack Coleman after Season Two when Corley grew frustrated with Steven's 'ever-shifting sexual preferences'. It has been suggested that the writers of the show succumbed to pressure from the Christian right-wing.

III: Limelink. (2018) *Visualizing Crowd Sizes*. Available at: blog.lime.link /visualizing-crowd-sizes/

V: '(Something Inside) So Strong' is a song by Labi Siffre, released in 1987.

Venus Infers: *L'esposizione del lenzuolo* (display of the sheet) is an old tradition in the South of Italy – rooted in women-shaming and patriarchy, no longer in practice – which involved the displaying of bloodstained sheets after the wedding night, to prove the bride's virginity and 'virtue'.

Acknowledgements

'Everything Is Named, Everything Is Counted' first appeared in *New Welsh Review*. 'Missing' and 'Don't Be A Stranger' first appeared in my pamphlet *Absolute Joy*.

A big thank you to Susie Wildsmith, editor and friend, and to all at Parthian. To Dan Lukins and all the Lufkin Poets, thank you for the continual warmth and support. To Cara Ludlow, who knows about words. To my mum, dad, Franco, Mark, and 'last but not least' to Siâni, thank you.

PARTHIAN *Poetry*

'Bert's writing, quite simply, makes me happy. Jealous but happy.' – CRYSTAL JEANS

Hey Bert
Roberto Pastore
ISBN 978-1-912109-34-0
£9.00 | Paperback

Highly Commended, Forward Prizes 2021

'…an impressive debut … This is profound poetry, spiritual and wise.'
– Frances Spurrier, *Wales Arts Review*

Hey Bert is a clarion call to open our eyes a little bit wider, of poetry's capacity to find new ways of looking at our own lives. Poems that speak intensely of the everyday, of nostalgia, friendship and love, the body, the sacred, all seen through Pastore's unique, eccentric filter of spirit animals, pop-culture, dreams and astrology.

Evoking John Giorno, Anne Waldman, and Julia Heyward, Pastore's work draws from performance art, confessional poetry, mantra, and folklore to create a voice both fiercely contemporary and somehow out of time.

PARTHIAN *Poetry*

Moon Base One
Jemma L. King
ISBN 978-1-917140-57-7

£10.00 | Paperback

'One of the most distinctive and exciting volumes of poetry to have come out of Wales in many years...'
– Jonathan Edwards on *The Undressed*

With exquisite lyricism and unflinching insight, *Moon Base One* is a meditation on survival, rebirth, and the ever-unfolding mystery of what it means to be alive.

Little Universe
Natalie Ann Holborow
ISBN 978-1-917140-21-8

£10.00 | Paperback

Shortlisted for Wales Book of the Year 2025

'This is intimate, poignant writing.' **– John McCullough**

Lives bustle within a busy hospital's walls, humming against the Gower landscape that stretches beyond its windows.

Breakfast with the Scavengers
Ben Rhys Palmer
ISBN 978-1-917140-56-0

£10.00 | Paperback

At once funny, tender, and beautifully bizarre, *Breakfast with the Scavengers* explores love, loss, loneliness, our never-ending quest for connection, and those blink-and-you-miss-them moments of transcendence that can light up our lives.

PARTHIAN *Poetry*

'One of Wales' most powerful young poetic voices'
WESTERN MAIL

BREAKING A MARE

CHRISTINA THATCHER

Breaking a Mare
Christina Thatcher
ISBN 978-1-917140-24-9
£10.00 | Paperback

'Thatcher wields form like a whip.' – *Mslexia*

Breaking a Mare is an investigation of silence, goodness and girlhood. It invites readers into the barn, the sawdust mill, the rodeo arena and asks what it means to be *good* in the face of physical, emotional and ecological threat.

Bathing on the Roof
Tracey Rhys
ISBN 978-1-917140-48-50
£10.00 | Paperback

'a fascinating exploration of femininity, power, and identity ... a standout.' – *Buzz Magazine*

'Rhys' voice is strong and expertly controlled, yet so often calm, contemplative and punctuated with such moments of beauty that I have been one moment swept away upon the tide, and in the next moment, have quieted, and have sighed.'
– **Jane Burn**

'Moving, funny, true and imbued with a gorgeous lyricism. Tracey Rhys's poems are the real thing. Highly recommended.' – Robert Minhinnick

Bathing on the Roof
TRACEY RHYS

'a lyrically inventive and unique voice' – Rhian Edwards